Princess things to make and do

Ruth Brocklehurst

Designed by Erica Harrison

Illustrated by Stella Baggott, Katie Lovell, Jan McCafferty,
Molly Sage and Josephine Thompson

Edited by Fiona Watt ★ Managing designer: Non Figg
Photographs by Howard Allman

Dancing princesses

You can paint lots of princesses, with different dresses and hairstyles, to make a large scene.

The white crayon lines are shown here in yellow so that you can see them.

The crayon lines stay white when you paint over the ballgown.

1. Draw the outline of a princess in a ballgown on a large piece of thick, white paper. Use a pencil and try not to press too hard.

2. Use a white wax crayon to draw frills and patterns on the ballgown. Then, draw wavy lines or curls for the hair.

3. Using a thick paintbrush, cover the piece of paper with water. Then, dip the brush in very watery paint and fill in the ballgown.

You could use white wax crayon and more watery paint to add a starry background to your scene.

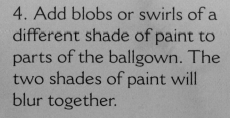

4. Add blobs or swirls of a different shade of paint to parts of the ballgown. The two shades of paint will blur together.

5. Fill in the hair with more watery paint. Use a thinner paintbrush to paint her crown, face and arms. Then, add the feet.

6. Leave the paint to dry completely. Then, use a sharp pencil to draw around the eyes, nose and mouth again.

Pretty princess headdress

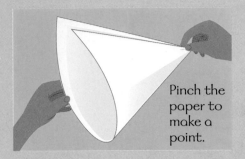

Pinch the paper to make a point.

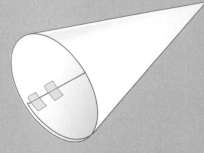

1. Draw half a circle on a large sheet of thick paper and cut it out. Bend the paper around and pinch the middle of the straight edge.

2. Wrap the curved edge of the semicircle around your head. Ask someone to slide one edge over the other until the cone fits neatly.

3. While the cone is on your head, ask someone to tape it together for you. Tape it on the outside, and then on the inside, too.

Overlap the pieces of tissue paper as you glue them on.

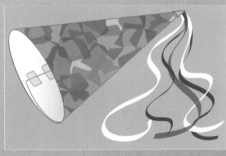

4. Rip different shades of tissue paper into small pieces. Brush glue over part of the cone at a time and press the pieces onto it.

5. Cover the whole cone in the same way. Then, cut several long strips of tissue paper or crêpe paper and tape them to the top.

6. Cut out two hearts from shiny paper. Then, glue them to the top of the cone, like this, to hide the sticky tape.

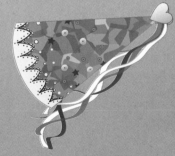

You may need to use hair clips to keep your headdress in place.

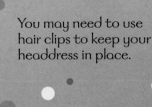

7. Paint a pretty border around the rim of your headdress. Then, decorate the cone with stickers, sequins or paper shapes.

Dainty slipper decorations

Make sure you press hard.

Don't cut along the inside lines.

1. Lay a piece of tracing paper over the template on this page and trace the sole template in pencil. Then, turn the tracing paper over.

2. Lay the tracing paper on a piece of thin cardboard. Draw over the lines to copy them onto the cardboard. Then, cut out the sole.

3. Trace the toe template and copy it onto a piece of thick paper in the same way. Then, cut out the toe shape.

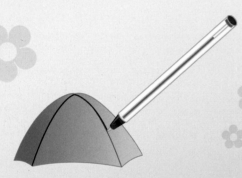

This is the template for the slipper.

The sole template is shown with a dotted line.

4. Using a ballpoint pen, draw along the lines on the toe. Press hard to make a crease. Then, fold the sides up along the creases.

The solid lines show the toe template.

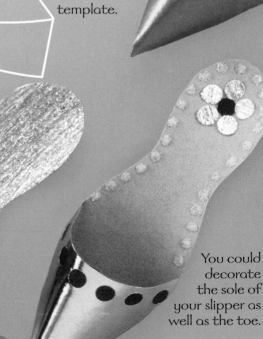

These slippers are for decoration, not for wearing.

5. Cut four slits in both folded sides of the toe to make tiny tabs. Fold the tabs along the creases so that they stand up.

You could decorate the sole of your slipper as well as the toe.

These slippers are shown actual size. You can use them to decorate your room or glue them to cards.

This slipper has a trim made from a cotton ball.

You could use some of the ideas on these slippers to decorate your slipper.

The tabs will overlap each other as you glue them on.

6. Put glue along the front edges of the base of the sole. Then, slide the sole under the right-hand tabs and press them on the glue.

7. With a finger inside the slipper, bend the toe around the sole. Then, press the left-hand tabs onto the glue.

8. Decorate the toe of the slipper with glitter, beads and shiny paper, or draw patterns on it with glitter glue or felt-tip pens.

Princess sash

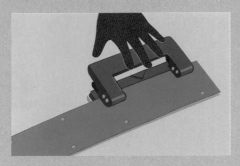

1. Cut a band of thin cardboard long enough to fit around your waist. Then, use a hole puncher to make holes along the long edges.

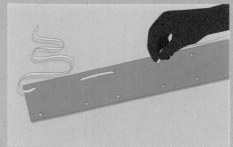

2. Cut two pieces of ribbon, twice as long as the sash. Thread one ribbon in and out of the holes along the top of the sash, like this.

Pull the ribbons so they dangle from both ends of the sash.

3. Thread the other ribbon through the holes along the bottom. Then, tape the ribbons at both ends of the sash, like this.

4. Draw lots of flowers, circles and tiny hearts on some different patterned wrapping papers. Then, cut them out.

5. Turn the sash over, so the tape is on the back. Then, glue the flowers, circles and hearts on the sash to decorate it.

6. To make the rosette, cut out a large flower from wrapping paper. Curl the edges of the petals by rolling each one around a pencil.

7. Cut two slightly smaller flowers, from different patterned papers. Make one smaller than the other. Curl their petals, too.

8. Glue the three flowers on top of each other in order of size, like this. Use a ballpoint pen to make two holes in the middle of them.

9. Thread a pipe cleaner through one of the holes. Turn the rosette over, bend the pipe cleaner and thread it through the other hole.

You can decorate your sash and rosette with sequins, beads and stickers, too.

10. Twist the ends of the pipe cleaner into spirals. Then, cut out a large leaf and tape it to the back of the rosette.

11. Glue the rosette near one end of the sash and leave the glue to dry. Then, tie the sash around your waist with the rosette to one side.

9

Zigzag castle card

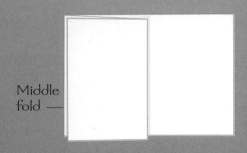

Middle fold —

Keep this part for later.

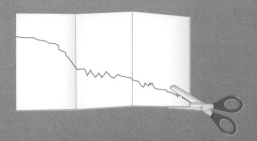

1. Fold a long rectangle of thick paper in half. Fold the top layer in half again, so the edge meets the middle fold, like this.

2. Turn the card over and fold it in the same way, to make a zigzag, then unfold the card. Cut off the left-hand section.

3. Using a pencil, draw a wavy line, diagonally across the card, as shown above. Then, cut along the line you have drawn.

You can decorate your zigzag cards with different styles of castles and all kinds of flowers.

4. Paint the right-hand part of the card green. When the paint is dry, paint tiny white and yellow flowers on it with a thin paintbrush.

5. Use purple paint to add mountains to the card. Leave the paint to dry. Then, outline the mountain peaks with a silver pen.

To make your card
stand up, pull the
front layer forward
to make a zigzag.

6. Turn the card over and
paint the middle part with
dark green paint. Then, cut
out trees from green paper
and glue them on.

7. Paint a castle on the
spare piece of paper. When
the paint is dry, add
outlines with a black pen.
Then, cut out the castle.

8. Fold the paper into a
zigzag again. Then, glue
the castle near the top of
the mountains, in the
middle of the card.

11

Queen's crown

Make the crosses taller than the points. Leave a plain part at each end.

Slit

1. Cut a long rectangle of thin cardboard that fits around your head, with a little overlap. Then, draw a line across the middle of it.

2. Draw points and crosses along the line, like this. Cut out the crown shape, then paint it gold or silver on both sides.

3. When the paint is dry, cut a slit going down, a little way from one end. Then, make another slit, going up, near the other end.

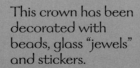

You can make differently shaped crowns, like this, too.

4. Bring the ends of the crown together. Slot them in place, with the ends inside, like this. Then, secure the ends with tape.

5. Cut eight little hearts from red paper and glue them to the crown. For a fur trim, glue cotton balls along the bottom.

This part is messy, so work on old newspapers.

This crown has been decorated with beads, glass "jewels" and stickers.

6. For jewels, roll eight pieces of foil into little balls. Cover the balls with household glue (PVA) and roll them in glitter.

7. Leave the jewels until they are completely dry. Then, glue them at equal spaces on the fur around the bottom of the crown.

8. Place a large plate on a piece of red crêpe paper or tissue paper and draw around it. Then, cut out the circle.

You will need to crumple the paper a little as you tape it.

9. Push the middle of the circle through the crown from the bottom. Tape the edge of the circle inside the crown, like this.

Lacy fan

The crayon lines are shown here in yellow so that you can see them.

1. Using a white crayon, draw lots of swirly lines on a large piece of white paper. Fill the paper with the shapes.

2. Then, cover the paper with pale, watery paint. While it is wet, paint a wide band of a different shade across the middle.

3. Paint two narrower dark stripes along the top and bottom of the paper. The darker stripes will blur into the pale background.

You could decorate your fan even more with gold or silver pen, or glitter, like the ones shown here.

4. When it is dry, fold the left-hand edge of the paper in by the width of two fingers. Turn the paper over and do the same again.

Be careful not to cut all the way across.

5. Keep folding and turning until the paper is folded. Cut a tiny triangle out of each end. Then, cut triangles along one edge.

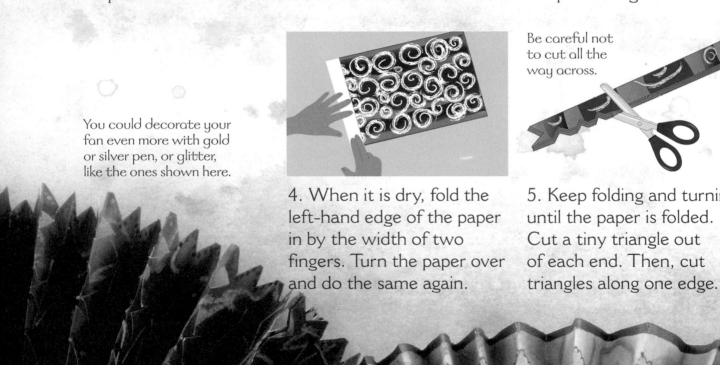

6. Fold the fan in half and unfold it again. Glue half of the fan. Then, fold the fan again, pressing the two sides firmly together.

7. For a handle, cut a strip of cardboard that is over twice the height of the fan. Fold the strip in half, then unfold it again.

Cut the strip the same width as the fan.

8. Glue the folded fan to one end of the strip. Spread glue over the rest of the strip and fold it in half to meet the top of the fan.

You can cut different sizes and shapes of holes in your fans to make more elaborate patterns.

9. Squeeze the two sides of the folded strip together firmly to make a handle below the fan. Then, open out the fan.

Sparkly tiara

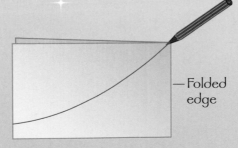

— Folded edge

1. Cut a long rectangle of thick paper that is long enough to fit around your head, with a little overlap. Then, fold it in half.

2. Using a pencil, draw a curved line across the paper. The pencil line should go to the top corner of the folded edge.

3. Using the first pencil line as a guide, draw curly lines on the paper, like this. Then, carefully cut along the curly lines.

Slit

4. Unfold the paper. Cut a slit going down, a little way from one end. Then, cut another slit, going up, near the other end.

This tiara was made by drawing slanted lines in step 3, instead of curly lines.

5. Decorate the tiara with gold and silver pens, stickers, beads and sequins. Then, slot the ends together, like this.

16

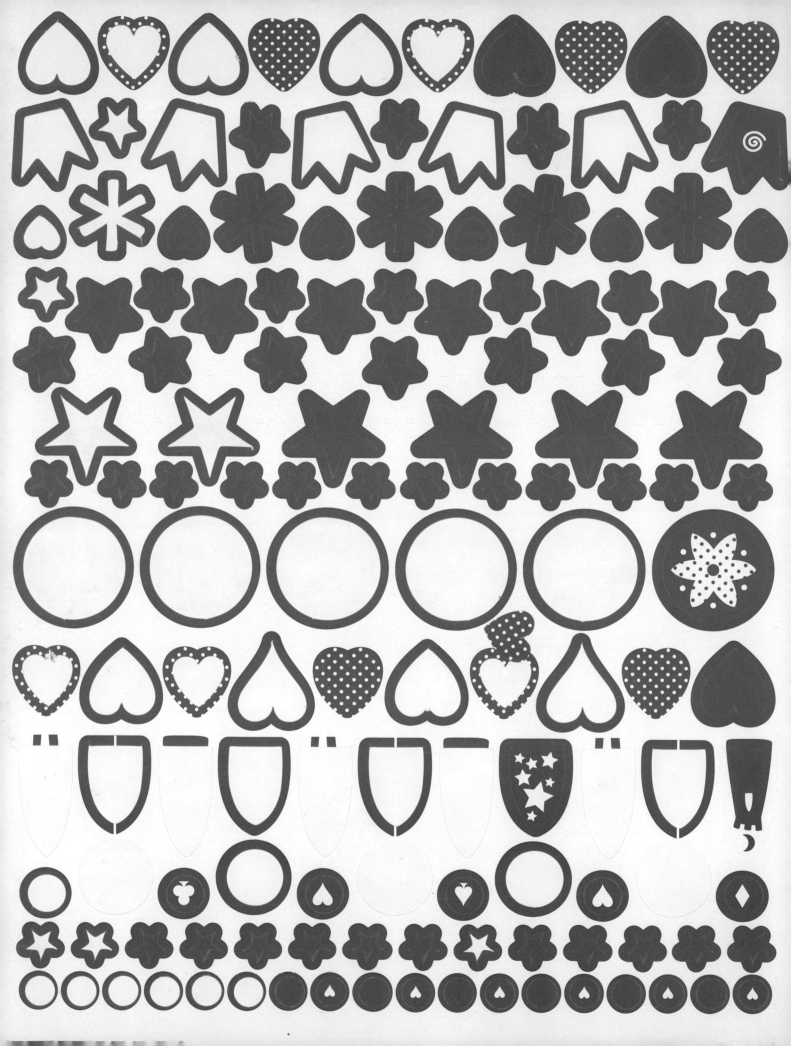

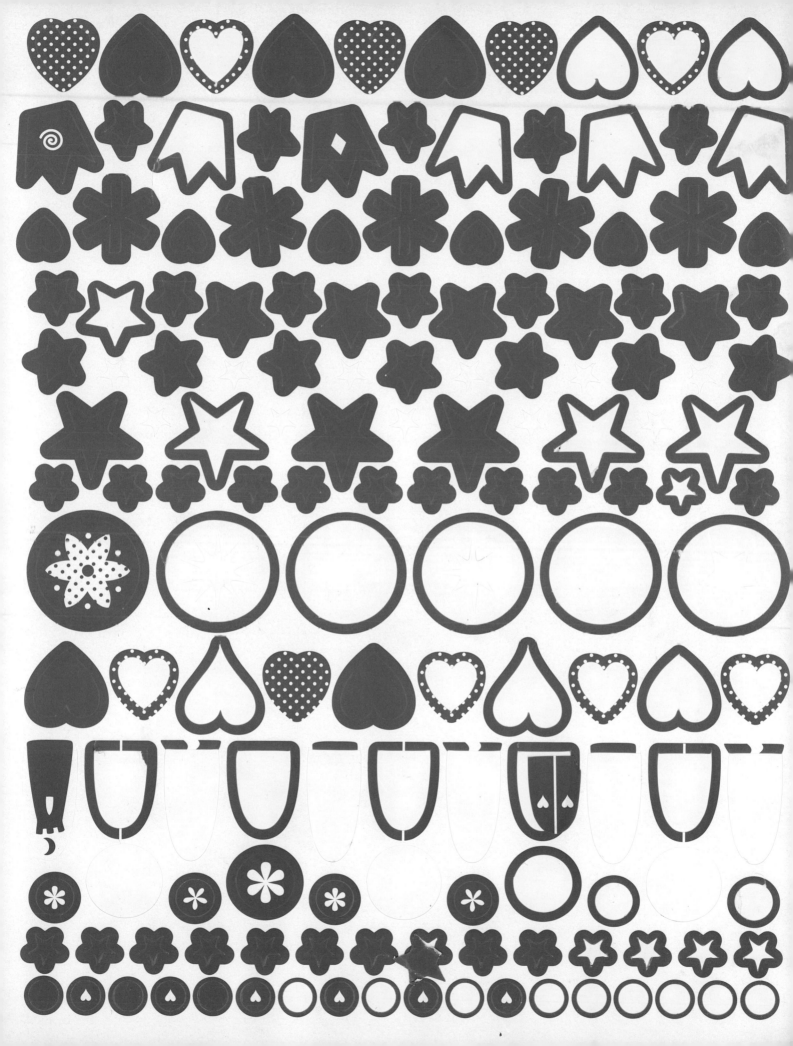

Princess in the tower bookmark

1. Draw the outline of a tower on a piece of blue cardboard. Make the tower wider at the top than at the bottom. Then, cut it out.

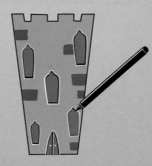

2. Use blue paint to add bricks to the tower and darker blue for windows and a tiny door. Then, outline them with pens.

When you use your bookmark, the princess will slot over the page and look out of the top of your book.

The shapes should overlap slightly.

3. Draw a circle and a curved shape, like this, on another piece of cardboard. These are for the head and shoulders of the princess.

4. Add long hair, a crown, and her clothes. Then, paint the princess. When the paint is dry, use a pen to add her face and outlines.

5. Cut out the princess. Slot the hair over the top of the tower. Then, tape her body to the back of the tower.

Fancy flags

These flags have been decorated with crowns and symbols copied from playing cards.

You could use bright thread or nylon fishing wire to hang your flags on.

1. For a flag template, mark the middle points of each edge of a rectangle of cardboard. Join the dots, then cut out the shape.

2. Place the cardboard template on some bright crêpe paper and draw around it in pencil. Then, cut out the shape.

3. Make several flag shapes, in different shades of crêpe paper, in the same way. Then, fold them all in half, like this.

You can add sparkle
to your flags by using
shiny paper or putting
glitter on them.

4. Cut out lots of small
crowns, hearts, diamonds
and fancy shapes. Glue the
shapes to the fronts of the
folded flags.

5. Cut out some even
smaller shapes and glue
them on top of the first
ones. Then, unfold all the
flags you have made.

6. Spread a flag with glue.
Lay a piece of thread over
the crease and fold the flag
over it. Then, glue the rest
of the flags onto the thread.

Princess door sign

Don't cut along this line.

1. Lay a small plate or bowl near the top of a long piece of thin cardboard. Then, draw around the plate or bowl with a pencil.

2. Draw two lines from the circle to the bottom of the cardboard. Lay the lid of a small jar in the middle of the circle and draw around it.

3. Draw two lines from the small circle to the edge of the larger circle, like this. Then, cut out the door sign shape, along the pencil lines.

Sleeping beauty
do not disturb

You could give your princess a fancy nightdress and a kitten, like this one.

Overlap the pillows as you glue them on.

4. Cut three large pillows from wrapping paper or an old magazine. Then, glue them across the sign, below the round hole.

If the hair is wider than the sign, trim off the edges.

5. Draw a big hairstyle on some magazine paper with hair texture on it and cut it out. Then, glue the hair across the pillows.

Glue the face over the neck and shoulders.

6. Draw a face, neck and shoulders on some paper. Cut them out and glue them to the hair, like this. Then, add a crown, too.

Trim the edges of the blanket to fit the sign.

7. For a blanket, cut a large piece of paper and glue it below the princess. Rip a strip of paper and glue it on top, then trim the edges.

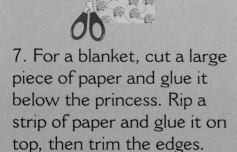

8. Cut out two arms and sleeves and glue them on, like this. Glue on a flower, too. Then, write a message on the top of the sign.

Princess Rose's room

Regal rosettes

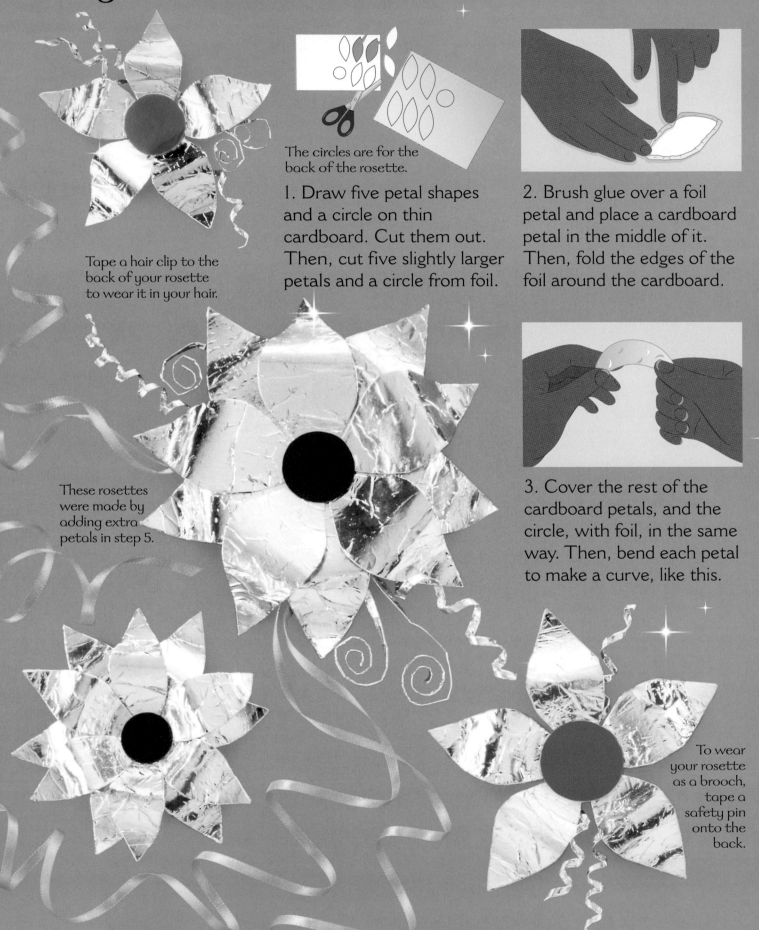

Tape a hair clip to the back of your rosette to wear it in your hair.

The circles are for the back of the rosette.

1. Draw five petal shapes and a circle on thin cardboard. Cut them out. Then, cut five slightly larger petals and a circle from foil.

2. Brush glue over a foil petal and place a cardboard petal in the middle of it. Then, fold the edges of the foil around the cardboard.

These rosettes were made by adding extra petals in step 5.

3. Cover the rest of the cardboard petals, and the circle, with foil, in the same way. Then, bend each petal to make a curve, like this.

To wear your rosette as a brooch, tape a safety pin onto the back.

4. Roll one end of a curved petal around a pencil, like this, to make it curl up. Then, do the same to the rest of the petals.

Use household glue (PVA).

5. Dab a blob of glue in the middle of the silver circle. Then, press the petals, foil side facing up, into the glue, to make a flower.

6. For tendrils, cut three strips of foil and roll them, to make thin sticks. Then, wind the sticks around a pencil to make coils.

7. Tape the coiled tendrils to the back of the rosette. Then, glue a small circle of purple paper in the middle of the rosette.

These tendrils were made by winding foil sticks (see step 6) into spiral shapes.

This rosette has been made with lots of layers of foil and patterned paper.

To make a patterned rosette like this, follow steps 6–10 on pages 8–9.

23

Swish bag

You don't need this part, but you will need the handles.

Don't draw around the handles.

1. Flatten a paper sandwich bag and use a ruler to draw a line across it, like this. Cut along the line, through all the layers of the bag.

2. Cut the handles off the top of the bag. Paint them, and the sides of the bag, red. When the paint is dry, tape the handles on.

3. Lay the bag on a piece of thin red cardboard. Draw around it twice and cut out both rectangles. Glue one to the back of the bag.

The lid of a spice jar is a good size.

The circles on your bag will swish as you carry it.

4. Draw around the lid of a small jar to make lots of circles on pieces of red, pink and gold cardboard or thick paper. Then, cut them out.

You could make a little purse like this to match your bag.

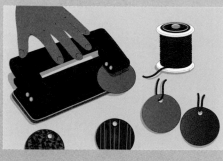

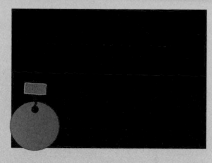

The number of circles you need will depend on the size of your bag.

5. Use a hole puncher to make a hole near the edge of each circle. Then, push a short thread through the hole in each circle.

6. With the thread at the top, lay one circle in the bottom corner of the spare red rectangle, like this. Tape the thread in place.

7. Tape more circles all along the bottom of the rectangle, in the same way. They should overlap each other slightly at the sides.

8. Tape another row of circles above the first row, so each circle hangs over the one below it. Add more rows to fill the rectangle.

9. Then, glue the decorated rectangle to the front of the bag. For a fur trim, glue cotton balls and sequins along the top of the bag.

You can decorate your bag with hearts or a bow, too.

Royal banquet collage

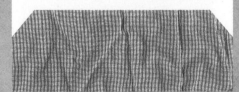

The tablecloth should slope in at the sides.

1. Cut out lots of different photographs of food – especially cakes, exotic fruit and party food – from old magazines.

2. Cut a large piece of patterned paper for a tablecloth. Then, glue it along the bottom of a big piece of paper.

3. Using a pencil, draw the outlines of two thrones behind the table. Then, draw a king and queen sitting on the thrones.

You could paint a bright background on your collage, too.

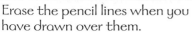
Erase the pencil lines when you have drawn over them.

4. Draw a prince and princess, next to the king and queen. Add a little dog, too. Then, go over the pencil lines with a black pen.

5. Arrange the photographs of food as though they are piled high on the tablecloth. Then, glue all the pictures in place.

6. When the table is full of food, paint the king, queen, prince and princess. Add details, such as jewels or buttons to their clothes.

Sweetheart chandelier

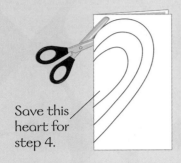

Save this heart for step 4.

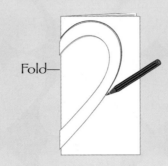

Fold—

1. Fold a large piece of thin cardboard in half. Draw half a heart against the fold, then draw two more half hearts inside. Cut along all the lines.

2. Fold another piece of thin cardboard in half. Lay the largest shape along the fold, like this, and draw around it. Then, cut it out.

3. Follow step 2 to make two more folded hearts, then unfold them all. Then, cut out nine small hearts. Lay them all on newspaper.

Cover the middle heart and a small one with red glitter. Do the rest pink.

4. Unfold the middle heart from step 1, too. Glue each shape and sprinkle them with glitter. Glitter the back of the small hearts, too.

5. Cut a piece of silver thread about the height of one of the large hearts. Then, cut nine pieces that are about half the length.

6. Glue a small heart onto each short thread. Then, tape the threads of two of the pink hearts onto each large heart, like this.

The chandelier will hang from this loop.

Make sure the edges and the folds match.

7. Glue the bigger red heart to the long thread. Fold the thread over, to make a loop. Then tape it to the top of one large pink heart.

8. Spread glue on the left-hand half of the heart. Fold another large heart in half, glitter sides in. Then, press one half of it onto the glue.

9. Fold the other two large hearts and glue them on in the same way. Then, tape the small red heart to the bottom of the chandelier.

When it is hung up, your chandelier will shimmer as it moves.

10. Spread glue on the bare half of the last large heart you glued on. Fold it over and press it onto the right-hand heart.

11. Pick up your chandelier. Then, crease the large folded hearts around the loop and at the bottom, to make them stand out evenly.

Printed giftwrap and cards

1. Cut two thick slices from the middle of a large potato. Then, dab them on both sides with paper towels to dry them.

2. Press a fork into a potato slice to make a handle. Spread thick paint on some paper towels. Then, dip the potato into the paint.

3. Press the potato onto a piece of paper. Dip it into the paint again to print more shapes. Keep printing until you have filled the paper.

You could print cards, with envelopes and note paper to match.

4. For a crown shape, cut the edges off the other slice of potato. Then, cut two small triangles from the top of the shape.

5. Press a fork into the crown and dip it into another shade of thick paint. Print a crown on each potato print on the paper.

More ideas

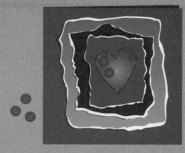

Try printing different shapes. You can use cookie cutters to cut out more difficult shapes, such as stars or hearts.

To make sparkly prints, use household glue (PVA) instead of paint and sprinkle it with glitter. Then, tip away the excess glitter.

For cards or gift tags, tear around a printed shape and glue it to another piece of paper. You could glue beads or sequins onto it, too.

Royal picture frame

Cut the strips slightly wider than the frame.

1. Place your picture in the middle of a rectangle of thick paper and draw around it. Put your picture to one side for later.

2. Make a hole in the middle of the rectangle with a ballpoint pen. Then, push scissors into the hole and cut around the pencil line.

3. Cut three strips of thick cardboard for the bottom and sides of the frame. Then, glue them to the paper frame.

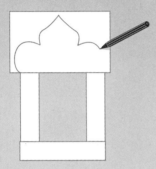

4. Draw a pretty arch that fits on the top of the frame, like this. Then, cut out the arch and glue it to the frame.

Gold paint has been brushed on top of the purple paint to make this frame look old.

5. Cut out lots of cardboard shapes and glue them to the frame. Then, paint the finished frame, and tape your picture to the back.

Photographic manipulation by Nick Wakeford • Images of flowers on pages 8-9, 20-21 and 23 © Digital Vision
This edition first published in 2011 by Usborne Publishing Ltd., 83-85 Saffron Hill, London, EC1N 8RT, England www.usborne.com
Copyright © 2011, 2004 Usborne Publishing Ltd. The name Usborne and the devices ♀☺ are Trade Marks of Usborne Publishing Ltd. All rights reserved.
No part of this publication may be reproduced, stored in a retrieval system, or transmitted in any form or by any means, electronic, mechanical,
photocopy, recording or otherwise, without prior permission of the publisher. This edition first published in America in 2011. UE. Printed in Malaysia.